Journal of a Duck's Midwife

Judith Wurtman

LEAPYEAR
PRESS

Acknowledgements

It may not take a condo community to hatch ducklings, but were it not for the spontaneous and eager help of my neighbors and the staff of the Heritage on the Garden, the process might have been unsuccessful. Since Sadie cannot or will not express her gratitude for the shelter provided by the plants that surrounded her nest, I will. Daryl Swartz, the head major-domo, whose immediate donation of two small evergreen trees gave the semblance of a concealed nesting area and relieved my worry that the duck would be too cold, wet, hot, or dry. My next door neighbor, Phyllis Meyer, also contributed plants to the nesting area and, along with Daryl, reassured me that the eggs would not become hard boiled. Wilder Nolasco—thank you for your inventive use of a screen door to block the ducklings from falling off the ledge of the balcony. And thank you Julie Drucker, for introducing me to Claudia, so many years earlier, while we were in the Boston Public Garden waiting for our dogs to pee. Little did I know that years later, this woman who chatted to us while feeding the squirrels, would be essential in helping to bring Sadie's ducklings to life and to a life with their mother on the Charles River. Thank you Claudia.[1] At the time of delivery, Sadie, Claudia and I were assisted by the wildlife rehabilitation expert Stephanie Ellis, Executive Director of Wild Care, Inc.[2]

Working with my editor, Marc Alonso, made transforming my journal and photographs into this book a joyous and often humorous endeavor. He is not only a brilliant editor of words, but also of pictures. Sadie and I thank him for making her look so good.

And finally, thanks to my husband Dick, my daughter Rachael and my grandchildren, Dvora and Jacob who visited Sadie often and told her what a good job I was doing.

1   https://www.facebook.com/GoldenBoughWildlife1/
2   https://www.wildcarecapecod.org

SUNDAY, MAY 23 WAS SUNNY and exceptionally warm for a Boston spring day. It was warmer than Miami Beach which we had left that morning. The apartment felt stuffy even though we turned on the air conditioner soon after we arrived home.

"I'll open up the door to the balcony," I told my husband who was busy going through the mounds of mail left in the little hall near the front door. He nodded as he carried stacks of advertisements out to the hall trash barrel.

The balcony was full of empty plant containers and three chairs stacked up against one of the brick walls of the building.

"Time to do some planting," I said to Chana, our mini black and white long-haired Dachshund as she systemically ran her nose over the concrete pavers.

The balcony was small; three people sitting there was really a crowd. It was bounded by two walls of the building and two, eight-foot railings attached to a ledge about three feet above the floor. Something brown was moving inside a terracotta planter on the far side of the tiny balcony.

What could it be?

I didn't think a squirrel or—*ugh*—a rat, could make the journey to the twelfth floor from the Public Garden across the street where they lived.

It was a duck—a female duck, her body ballooned to occupy the entire planter. What was she doing here? *How did she get here?* Why the planter?

Don't frighten her, I thought and picking up Chana, quickly and quietly, left the balcony.

Now what?

There was no one to call on Sunday and trying to put worries about the duck out of my mind, I spent the rest of the day attempting to restore life to an apartment that seemed moribund from our winter stay in Florida. But I worried.

What mother wouldn't?

MONDAY, MAY 24.

THE SUN RISES EARLY IN MAY in Boston and I was wide awake by 5:15. Was the duck still there? Had it, like our flag, survived the night? Or more accurately, had *she?* I assumed she would be sitting on her eggs, but she was gone.

But *where* had she gone? Would she come back? Maybe she went to find something to eat or drink? To talk things over with papa?

When I looked up mating and hatching among mallards on Wikipedia, I found this: "Ducks generally only have one partner at a time, although the partnership usually only lasts one year. Larger species and the more sedentary species (like fast-river specialists) tend to have pair-bonds that last numerous years. Most duck species breed once a year, choosing to do so in favourable conditions (spring/summer or wet seasons). Ducks also tend to make a nest before breeding, and, after hatching, lead their duck-lings to water. Mother ducks are very caring and protective of their young, but may abandon some of their ducklings if they are physically stuck in an area they cannot get out of (such as nesting in an enclosed courtyard) or are not prospering due to genetic defects or sickness brought about by hypothermia, starvation, or disease. Ducklings can also be orphaned by inconsistent late hatching where a few eggs hatch after the mother has abandoned the nest and led her ducklings to water. Most domestic ducks neglect their eggs and ducklings, and their eggs must be hatched under a broody hen or artificially." [1]

When I looked again an hour or so later, she was back, staring at the walls of the planter and not—thank goodness—reacting when I tiptoed out onto the balcony to watch.

I have to get some advice. Whom should I call? Animal Rescue League? A wild life organization? Friends of water fowl? Is there such an organization?

I called the Animal Rescue League and someone there recommended I contact an animal rehabilitator, Claudia Travis. She was not someone who works in a detox center for animals, but someone who rescues orphaned urban wildlife like bunnies whose mothers were run over by motorized lawn mowers or baby squirrels who fall from their nests. I knew her; usually, she was at our end of the Boston Public Garden around sunset, feeding the squirrels healthy food to compensate for the junk food most of people toss at them. She had given names to all the squirrels in her care and yes, they responded to her call. But who could tell? To me, they all looked alike.

---

[1]   https://en.wikipedia.org/wiki/Duck; retrieved 13 July, 2021.

I would watch her feed the squirrels while Simon, my recently departed long-haired Dachshund, sniffed every drop of pee within yards of his nose. Claudia and I would talk while Simon was away from the squirrels, off sniffing a patch of grass. One day, when I was walking Simon, I met Julie, a neighbor from my building who was walking her own dog. Claudia came over to us. She was laughing and pointing to a woman.

"That woman wanted to buy a squirrel," Claudia told us. "She asked me how much they cost. I explained to her that they were not for sale and that they live in the Garden and need to stay here."

"Why did she want a squirrel?" I asked, thinking that she was possibly a zany rich person who might make a big donation to the Public Garden. How many squirrels did the Garden really need anyway?

"She wanted to take one back home to show her children," Claudia told us.

"Why just one squirrel?" asked Julie. "If she had two, she could populate her neighborhood."

Claudia looked horrified until Julie and I started to laugh again.

When I finally got Claudia on the phone, she remembered me and expressed condolences when I told her Simon had died the previous September, at seventeen-and-a-half.

"Don't worry about the duck," she reassured me after I described the maternity ward on my deck. "Try to get some plants around the planter so she feels protected. And I will get you some food for her. And don't worry about having the duck see you. She needs to feel comfortable around people so she won't fly away after her ducklings are born."

When that happy day arrived, Claudia explained, we would not be making a procession from my balcony to the street, although the idea was delightfully appealing. Claudia would come with a helper and large nets; one for mama duck and the other for the ducklings. Her concern was that Mama would abandon the ducklings in her haste to avoid danger. She had seen this happen before, and unless another duck adopted them, the ducklings would die.

"If she is used to seeing humans, she might not be afraid," she told me.

Phyllis, who lives across the hall from me, gave me two almost dead house plants to put on the balcony.

"Throw them away when you don't need them anymore," she told me. The plants were about four feet high but had thin leaves and the two pots did not really conceal the duck from view. Daryl, our building's head concierge, said that he would check to see if anyone was throwing out plants. When he called again, he reported that he thought he could provide some, but not before Tuesday.

Before going to bed, I checked on the duck and found her fast asleep.

TUESDAY, MAY 26.

I LEFT THE HOUSE EARLY TO TAKE THE CAR to the dealership for its annual checkup and inspection. When I returned, all was quiet on the duck front. It was close to noon and it had taken an hour to walk back from Brookline. Daryl was waiting for me with two, five-foot-high pine trees in containers he had bought at Home Depot the night before. We put the trees around the duck's nest and suddenly, she was almost entirely concealed. As I walked away, I looked at the water in the dog bowl sitting on the ledge near her nest. It looked untouched.

Why wasn't she drinking?

Claudia called in the middle of the afternoon and said she had duck food for me. She would be in the park feeding the squirrels around 5:00, and I could get it from her then. When I found her, I wasn't sure if the bag she handed me contained duck food or Israeli couscous. But Claudia told me it was duck food and that I was to soak it in a lot of water, and add some thinly sliced bok choy or romaine lettuce before serving it to the duck. She said that I should also get organic vegetables from the pricey local market, but I decided to get the bok choy from a small supermarket in Chinatown. When I was finished preparing the food, it looked like an Asian soup. I resisted the temptation to add soy sauce. Only the best for Mama duck.

The first feeding went well and, in retrospect, more easily than subsequent ones. The duck hopped onto the wide shelf where empty planters were stacked and, dipping her beak into the water, ate. She slurped her food and it seemed she swallowed a fair amount of water. I thought of a visit to Japan many years before, where friends took me to lunch and demonstrated the Japanese noodle slurping technique. The duck was a natural at this.

WEDNESDAY, MAY 26.

T HE EARLY MORNING WEATHER FORECAST was for a very hot day. And so it was. By mid-afternoon, it was about ninety degrees and the sun beat down on the duck. I rigged an umbrella over her but the wind blew it over. Boston weather is not conducive to sitting on eggs in an exposed area.

There were thunderstorms around 9:00 AM and then heavy rain.

Must figure out how to attach an umbrella to the nesting area.

THURSDAY, MAY 27.

Duck's needs took second place to Chana. Drove Chana to Angell Memorial Hospital around 9:30 AM, feeling horribly guilty all the way there. I kept apologizing to her as she sat on my lap in the car. As the driver, I know this is bad, but she refuses to stay on the passenger side and hops into my lap even before I fasten my safety belt.

I surrendered her to a so-called "patient advocate" who promised to look after her. And she did, sending me a picture about an hour later and telling me that everyone was paying attention to Chana because she was so cute.

When I got back home, still feeling guilty, I fed the duck who I now call Sadie. Now, Sadie won't eat out of the dish I leave on the balcony ledge unless I hold it under her beak. She dips her beak into the water over and over again, but when she is finished, she pecks at my fingers so I will take the bowl away.

By late afternoon, I start to obsess over Chana's fate and, less so, the duck's.

Why hasn't the vet called me?

Chana's must have been spayed by now. *How long could this procedure take?* When I called Angell to ask how the patient was doing, I was told that Chana's vet and his assistant were not answering their pages. Visions of Chana bleeding out in the OR went through my head.

I must stop watching those medical dramas on television.

Just as I was considering driving back to the hospital and demanding to see my puppy, a text message arrived from Dr Brum's intern saying that Chana was awake and eating her dinner.

Now I can worry only about Sadie. I fed her before I went to sleep.

FRIDAY, MAY 28.

Picked up chana. She was sleepy and looked silly with her so-called Elizabethan collar around her neck. I am running out of duck food. I texted Claudia and she replied that her husband would leave a bag at the front desk of our building. Sadie seems to like bok choy, so I have been cutting it into small pieces and letting them float in the water with the duck pellets.

It is going to rain Friday night and the rain will continue through the upcoming Memorial Day weekend.

I must prevent the nest from getting wet.

My large, golf-size umbrella is big enough to cover most of the planter and I manage to anchor it by pushing the very heavy, stone gargoyle up against half of the opened umbrella and then pushing another part of the fabric under the wrought iron balustrade. The gargoyle—a reproduction of those at *Notre Dame* in Paris—must be made of stone because it is extremely heavy. I couldn't lift it but did manage to push it as close to the umbrella as possible. Unless the wind is strong, I think the umbrella will hold. And if not? Visions of concrete gargoyles with umbrellas flying from my balcony onto the balconies below me fill me with dread.

SATURDAY, MAY 29.

THE RAIN WAS COMING DOWN HARD when I woke up. I checked on Sadie right away. Though it was at 7:00 am, it was still very dark. She was gone.

Where is she?

There are eight, white eggs in the planter, but no mama. And it is really cold: thirty-nine degrees. How can the eggs stay viable?

I check every hour but no Sadie. When I take Chana outside late that morning for her second pee of the day, I bump into Daryl.

"The duck is gone," I tell him.

"Maybe she will come back," he reassures me.

I am not reassured.

SATURDAY, 2:00 PM.

THE DUCK IS BACK. *Where was she?*

I call Claudia and comment that this seems to be an exercise in futility. *Why have the duck sit on dead eggs?* Claudia tells me to wait until she checks with an authority on duck eggs (not a chef). She calls back and says that, according to this expert, the eggs may still be viable and that the duck may well be laying new ones.

New ones? I am going to be a midwife all summer?

SUNDAY, MAY 30.

ANOTHER COLD AND RAINY DAY. Feels like late November rather than the end of May. I propped up a second umbrella as more of a wind shield than protection from the rain. Mama Duck ate twice. She eats for no more than five minutes before she pecks at my fingers so I will leave her alone. Around 7:00 PM, when I was putting on my winter jacket and getting her food dish ready, I looked through the window at the planter and saw only eggs. She was gone again.

She was still gone by the time we went to bed.

Could she be a bigamist with another nest somewhere else?

MONDAY, MEMORIAL DAY.

R AIN NOT VERY HEAVY IN THE MORNING and stopped altogether by
mid afternoon.

Mama is back. She must be an optimist.

She was hungry and did a duck's version of gobbling the food each time I fed her.

This afternoon, I went to an outdoor plant shop in Somerville. It is time to put plants in the planters on the balconies and I bought enough to fill several pots. Hopefully, the flowers will cheer Sadie up enough that she won't abscond again.

Evening: she is gone again.

A party?

Tuesday, June 1.

S ADIE WAS BACK by daybreak.

It is warm today and instead of the dirty gray, rain filled clouds that plagued us all weekend, the sky is a light blue. I started potting my plants very early and was finished by 9:00. Sadie ignored me entirely. I offered her breakfast but she pecked at me.

Is she feeling peckish?

Sadie ate later on and frequently dipped her beak into the broth. She must have been thirsty. I fed her again about 4:00 and she ate. But she is not covering the eggs with her body. To my dismay, two and sometimes three eggs are exposed.

Why do I feel so responsible? Because I am a Jewish mother?

Friday, June 4.

Sadie knows me—at least she seems to know the sound of my voice—and although she puffs herself up when I sit beside her on the balcony, her feathers settle down after a few minutes. But she is not eating. I offer her food three times a day, but she is eating less and less. She dips her beak into the dish two or three times but then refuses to continue. When I jiggle the bowl, she becomes annoyed and pecks at my fingers but she never breaks the skin.

I am worried that she will be dehydrated. We are expecting another heat wave this weekend and it will be unbearably hot on the balcony. I think I'd better keep the umbrella over her to provide some shade.

Yesterday, I went into the gourmet grocery store at the end of Charles Street to get some marrow bones for Chana. While the butcher was pushing the bones through a noisy bone saw so they would be small enough for her to pick up with her mouth, I noticed duck eggs for sale in a refrigerated case.

I wonder if they would take three week old eggs on consignment?

FRIDAY EVENING.

I SAW CLAUDIA IN THE PARK tonight when I took Chana out.

"What am I supposed to do on day twenty-eight if the eggs don't hatch and Sadie is still here?" I asked.

"Not all the eggs may be that old," she told me. "She may have laid some more recently."

Good grief. Sadie may never leave. *What if the eggs don't hatch?*

Claudia said that an expert on duck eggs would come over around the twenty-eighth day to see if the eggs are viable. She didn't know what the technique was, but she thought it was something like holding a candle under the egg. I thought candling eggs is something people did a hundred years ago.

What about ultra sound?

Tuesday, June 8.

Very hot again, as it was yesterday. The bowl of food and water I left for Sadie was almost empty yesterday afternoon—but so was the nest. She was gone by early evening and now, almost twelve hours later, she still is not back. The eggs are covered with down but the ducklings inside may be dead by now.

Too bad. I was hoping that we would have ducklings.

Friday, June 11. Morning.

WEATHER HAS CHANGED and now it is cool. I met Claudia and her husband Malcolm in the park yesterday around 6:00 PM. Claudia was feeding the squirrels and told me about a sparrow that had been attacked and wounded by an off-leash dog. She was very upset because the bird was probably going to die.

After Chana was done with her business, we went back to our building and Claudia and her husband came by about thirty minutes later. Claudia looked at the balcony and suggested that we try to find some way of preventing the ducklings from falling off the balcony.

Falling off the balcony?

The railing, which is intended to protect a human body from falling, is not narrow enough to prevent someone tiny like a duckling from slipping between the rails and falling. I think I can find some netting at Home Depot, but I will wait until there are some cracks in the eggs. No point in rigging something to protect the ducklings if there are no ducklings.

I made fresh food for Sadie this morning and she ate a little, but not enough to nourish her. Good thing she doesn't have to breast feed her ducklings.

SUNDAY, JUNE 13.

ANOTHER BEAUTIFUL DAY. This is the start of week four. Of course, I don't actually know how long she had been on the balcony. She may have passed her twenty-eighth day by now. There is nothing I can do but wait.

She is not eating much or drinking, and I worry that she is going to get sick. If nothing happens by mid-week, I will ask Claudia to test the eggs.

MONDAY, JUNE 14.

T HE DAY STARTED OUT clear and dry but by 10:00 am, the rain started and it has poured off and on all day. When the rain had stopped around 2:00, I managed to go outside onto the balcony to feed Sadie. She was hungry and thirsty but stopped drinking after a few minutes.

Suddenly, she shifted her position and I saw a square opening in one of her eggs and something dark inside. Another egg next to it was cracked but not yet open. Sadie quickly moved to cover the eggs, but I nudged her a little to check again to assure myself that the egg had an opening—that I wasn't imagining it.

Uh oh!

The ducklings are going to be born, and I never did figure out how to cover the railings!

I ran to find Nicole who is the concierge on duty and asked her if I could get some some plastic bin liners. I thought that if the plastic was taped around the railings, the ducklings would be protected, but one of the maintenance people had a better idea. Wilder, who is an extremely creative person, brought up two screened doors that had been discarded. They were very light and he was able to prop them on the ledge and secure them to the railing with a stretchy plastic cord. They covered the railings and I felt very much relieved once he had finished.

I called Claudia. Did I sound like a new father about to leave for the hospital with his wife in labor? Probably. Claudia did not think the screens would work because the mother duck could fly over them and leave her ducklings behind.

Of course.

Her solution was to enclose the planter in a sort of pen, so when the ducklings are born, neither they nor their mother can escape.

She went to a pet supply store and bought a large dog pen, sort of like a dog playpen. It was soft sided so if the ducklings bumped into it, they wouldn't be hurt. A panel that could be unzipped was on either side of the enclosure so we could reach inside to grab Mama and the ducklings. Claudia inverted the pen over the planter and, although it was rather dark inside, it was also a safe space.

LATER ON THAT EVENING, it rained heavily but the pen kept the duck dry.

"When do you think they will be born?" I asked Claudia for the fifteenth time, or so it seemed. She kept revising the time upwards.

"It may take at least twelve hours, maybe twenty-four," she told me.

That meant that I didn't have to get up every few hours during the night to check, but I found a flashlight and put it near the door to the balcony. If I was up in the middle of the night, why not check on the progress of the births?

I did. *Nothing.*

Fare Well

CLAUDIA AND STEPHANIE ARRIVED at our apartment at 8:00 this morning. Stephanie is a water fowl expert and she drove from the Cape early this morning to help Claudia. We went out onto the balcony and Stephanie unzipped one of the panels near the planter to check on Sadie. She quickly lifted her, put her back, and grinned at us.

"She is sitting on a heap of wet, squirming ducklings!" she told us. "No eggs—just ducklings."

They were born.

All of them.

I found it hard to believe. We all grinned at each other. I went over to Sadie and whispered, *Mazel Tov.*

There followed a long discussion about what to do.

"The ducklings need to dry," Stephanie said. "It could take several hours." And sadly, she had to return to the Cape.

Claudia said she would return with her husband in the early afternoon to take the family to the Charles River. We all decided that even though the duck had probably been living across the street in the duck pond, she needed a quieter, safer place to raise her ducklings. The Boston Public Garden was wall-to-wall people, dogs, children, and geese every weekend—there were few places for a duck family to be concealed.

I checked on Sadie and her brood every hour or so, and around 11:30, saw two fluffy yellow ducklings peeking out from under Sadie. I could just make out the head of a third, but they all retreated under Mama. My visions of ducklings cavorting in the pen were just that: visions and wishful thinking. The ducklings stayed put.

Claudia arrived with Malcolm and prepared for Operation Duck Removal. Sticking her head inside the pen, she grabbed at Sadie who, predictably, flew off, very agitated. Claudia kept crawling until her whole body was inside the pen, and she managed to grab the duck who flapped her wings and squawked and let loose a torrent of poop. It got all over the floor, the pen, the dishes inside the pen and Claudia's hands and clothes.

"Well," said Claudia, "I guess she has been eating."

Somehow, she held onto the duck and managed to push her into the crate. Then, one by one, she picked up the ducklings and put them into the crate, closed it, and put a blanket on top that Stephanie had left with us and then went to wash herself.

We counted seven ducklings. Later on, it turned out that the eighth had been injured during the attempt to move Sadie. Its body was found a few hours later when the pen was cleaned.

Claudia carried the box, whose soft sides wiggled, as Sadie thumped her displeasure. Malcolm, Dick and I followed them into the elevator and

down to the fifth floor. We proceeded down the hall to the central elevator. Residents and staff people congratulated us as we passed.

It was not quite *Make Way for Ducklings,* but it was a parade of sorts nevertheless.

The transfer to the car was quick. Malcolm sat in back with the crate and I rode next to Claudia. There was little traffic and we reached the Charles River, where it bends toward Watertown, in about fifteen minutes. Claudia pulled into the parking lot behind the Community Boating house. No one was around and even the river was quiet. No boats, no kayaks.

We walked to the river bank and Claudia took Sadie out of the crate and placed her close to the water. Meanwhile, I removed the ducklings, one by one, and put them on the ground near the water. They were soft and sweet. I wanted to hold them, but I was afraid that Sadie might reject them if I touched them for more than a few seconds.

Sadie took off, paddling away from us.

"Where are you going?" we asked, dismayed by her imminent disappearance.

What do we do if she doesn't come back?

But a few seconds later, she turned, paddled to the shore and walked over to the ducklings. Some invisible signal (invisible to us) made them line up like toddlers at a day-care center, out for their walk. As they walked behind her, one fell and lay upside down on the bank. Sadie turned and nudged the duckling upright. A few minutes—maybe even seconds—and all were in the Charles. Barely six hours old, seven ducklings swam with their mother. Sadie's neck was erect, her head high. She looked like the duck equivalent of Queen Victoria, with all her children paddling behind her.

I watched her gliding away and thought, there is a mother who endured what must have been a very unpleasant twenty-eight days: temperatures that ranged from very hot to very cold, pelting rain, blazing sun, nuisance noise from humans, dogs, traffic, synthetic duck food pushed under her nose in a metal bowl by a large human, gigantic umbrellas erected over her nest, a small dog sniffing the planter and a parade of curious visitors, all of whom wondered how she managed to get to the twelfth floor.

And just when her confinement is over, when her offspring emerged, and she was free, a strange woman comes along, pushes her into a crate with her ducklings, puts them into a car and drives away. She is miles from her home on the Duck Pond, where no doubt, the father of her children is hanging out with his Mallard buddies. Finally, she is deposited in an unfamiliar part of the Charles River, where she doesn't recognize any of the other ducks hanging around the bank.

But then, she is in the water. Her children, all seven, follow behind her, paddling as if they have been doing it for months, rather than only minutes. She does a victory lap to the other side of the river, shining silver under the bright June sun.

And I, the pesky human, her midwife, turn away, tears in my eyes.

Unbidden, the Jewish prayer, the *shehecheyanu* forms on my tongue. It is a prayer recited after one experiences something new or unusual.

Blessed are You Lord our God, Ruler of the Universe who has given us life, sustained us, and allowed us to reach this day.

I breathed a sigh of relief.

And have a happy, safe life.

I caught up to Claudia and as we walked to the car, I started singing: *"Be kind to your web footed friends…"*

Without missing a beat, she continued: *"For that duck may be some-body's mother!"*

We laughed and hugged and turned to look at Sadie somewhere on the river.

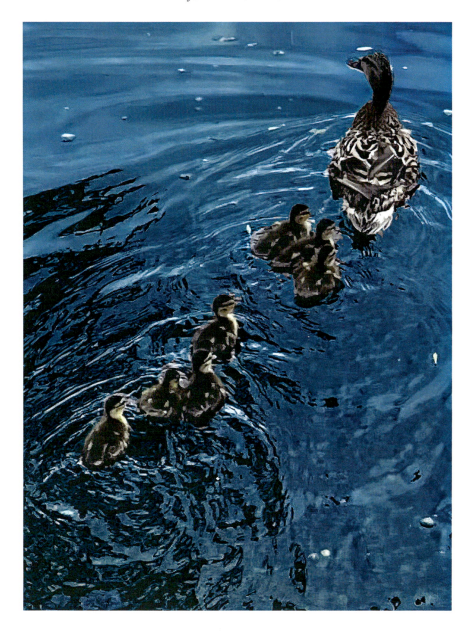